# ANNECY TRAVEL GUIDE

2(

Explore Attractions, Insider's Tips, and Itineraries.

Amy F. Prather

## Copyright © 2025 by (Amy F. Prather)

All rights reserved. No part of this publication may be reproduced, distributed, or transmitted in any form or by any means, including photocopying, recording, or other electronic or mechanical methods, without the prior written permission of the publisher, except in the case of brief quotations embodied in critical reviews and certain other noncommercial uses permitted by copyright right.

# TABLE OF CONTENTS

**INTRODUCTION**   7
    An Overview of the Region in Brief   9
    Why Visit Annecy?   13
**CHAPTER 1:**   16
**PLANNING YOUR TRIP**   16
    Best Time to Visit   17
    Getting to Annecy   18
    Getting Around Annecy   20
    What to Pack   21
    Entry and Visa Information   22
    Currency and Language   23
    Budget Travel Tips   24
    Money-Saving Hacks   25
    Where to Book Your Trip   26
**CHAPTER 2:**   27
**TOP ATTRACTIONS AND LANDMARKS**   27
    1. Old Town (Vieille Ville) - The City Center   28
    2. Palais de l'Île - An Iconic Landmark   29
    3. Château d'Annecy - A Castle with a View   30
    4. Lake Annecy - A Pristine Water Gem   31
    5. Pont des Amours (Lovers' Bridge) - A Romantic   32
    6. Jardins de l'Europe - A Relaxing Green Space   33
    7. The Thiou Canal - A Waterway with Character   34
    8. Basilica of the Visitation - A Spiritual and Architectural Gem   35
    9. Mont Veyrier - A Hiker's Viewpoint   36
    10. Day Trips from Annecy   37
**CHAPTER 3:**   38
**ACCOMMODATION OPTIONS**   38

| | |
|---|---|
| Types of Accommodations Available | 39 |
| Top Hotels and Resorts (Luxury & Mid-Range Options) | 40 |
| Budget-Friendly Options (Affordable Stays) | 42 |
| Tips for Booking and Choosing Accommodation | 44 |
| **CHAPTER 4:** | **46** |
| **DINING AND CUISINE** | **47** |
| Local Cuisine and Popular Dishes | 49 |
| Best Restaurants in Annecy (For All Budgets) | 49 |
| Street Food and Local Eateries (Budget-Friendly Options) | 51 |
| Dining by the Lake (Scenic Outdoor Options) | 52 |
| **CHAPTER 5:** | **54** |
| **OUTDOOR ACTIVITIES AND ADVENTURE** | **54** |
| Hiking Trails Galore | 55 |
| Boat Tours and Water Adventures | 57 |
| Cycling Through the Countryside | 59 |
| Beach Bliss | 60 |
| Rock Climbing and Adventure Sports | 62 |
| **CHAPTER 6:** | **64** |
| **ART, CULTURE, AND ENTERTAINMENT** | **64** |
| Local Festivals and Events | 65 |
| Shopping and Markets | 67 |
| Nightlife and Entertainment Options | 69 |
| **CHAPTER 7:** | **73** |
| **A 7-DAY ITINERARY IN ANNECY** | **73** |
| Day 1: | 74 |
| Getting There and Seeing the Old Town | 74 |
| Day 2: | 76 |
| Outdoor Adventures & Boat Cruise | 76 |
| Day 3: | 78 |

| | |
|---|---|
| Château Visits & Cycling the Countryside | 78 |
| Day 4: | 80 |
| Outdoor Adventures and Nature's Wonders in Malaga | 80 80 |
| Day 5: | 82 |
| Day Trip to La Clusaz & Alpine Activities | 82 |
| Day 6: | 83 |
| Lakeside Relaxation & Hidden Spots | 83 |
| Day 7: | 84 |
| Farewell to Annecy | 84 |
| **CHAPTER 8:** | **85** |
| **PRACTICAL INFORMATION AND TIPS** | **85** |
| Etiquette and Customs | 86 |
| Language and Communication | 88 |
| Health and Safety Tips | 91 |
| Emergency Contacts | 92 |
| Communication and Internet Access | 93 |
| Useful Apps, Websites, and Maps | 94 |
| **CONCLUSIONS** | **96** |

# INTRODUCTION

The first time I visited Annecy, I didn't know what to expect. I had seen photos of its crystal-clear lake, winding canals, and stunning mountain backdrop, but nothing compared to seeing it in person. I remember sitting by the water, watching kayakers glide across the surface as the sun sparkled on the waves. The air was fresh, the streets were full of life, and the food was unforgettable. That moment stayed with me. I knew I had to return, uncover more, and share this incredible town with others.

Each visit to Annecy has brought discoveries. From stumbling upon a quiet café in the Old Town to hiking to panoramic viewpoints or witnessing the dazzling Fête du Lac fireworks, every trip deepened my appreciation for this remarkable place. Annecy isn't just another travel destination—it's a place that draws you in, whether you're traveling solo, seeking a romantic getaway, or planning a family adventure.

That's why I wrote this guide. My goal is to help you explore Annecy like a local, avoid tourist traps, and make the most of your time here. With insider tips and personal recommendations, this book will give you everything you need to plan an unforgettable trip.

So whether you're still dreaming about visiting or already packing your bags, let's dive into Annecy's charm, uncover its hidden treasures, and create lasting memories. By the time you finish this guide, I hope you'll not only be prepared for your trip but also inspired to chase your travel adventures—wherever they may lead.

# An Overview of the Region in Brief

Annecy is a breathtaking lakeside town in the French Alps, known for its stunning landscapes, rich history, and lively atmosphere. Often called the "Venice of the Alps," it's famous for its clear blue lake, scenic canals, and historic Old Town filled with cobblestone streets and colorful buildings.

### Location & Geography

Located in southeastern France, Annecy sits in the Haute-Savoie region of Auvergne-Rhône-Alpes. It lies at the northern tip of Lake Annecy, one of Europe's cleanest lakes, thanks to strict environmental protections. Surrounded by mountains, it's a paradise for outdoor enthusiasts all year round.

### Where History Meets Modern Charm

Annecy's roots trace back to the Roman era, but it flourished in the Middle Ages as a key trade and religious center. Today, it seamlessly blends medieval characters with modern attractions. The Old Town (Vieille Ville) is a maze of canals, bridges, and historic architecture, while the surrounding areas offer trendy shops, ski resorts, and nature trails.

**A Year-Round Destination**

- Spring & Summer: Perfect for boating, swimming, and cycling along the lake. Markets and festivals fill the streets with energy.

- Autumn: A quieter season with breathtaking fall colors and fewer crowds.

- Winter: A gateway to ski resorts like La Clusaz and Le Grand-Bornand, just a short drive away. The town comes alive with Christmas markets and festive lights.

**Culture & Local Life**

Annecy is a hub for art, film, and outdoor activities. Every June, it hosts the renowned Annecy International Animation Film Festival, and in August, the Fête du Lac (Lake Festival) lights up the sky with one of Europe's most spectacular fireworks displays. Food lovers will enjoy local specialties like tartiflette (a cheesy potato dish) and fresh fish from the lake.

Whether you're here for adventure, relaxation, or culture, Annecy offers something for everyone. In the following chapters, we'll explore the best ways to experience this incredible town.

# Why Visit Annecy?

Annecy isn't just a beautiful town—it's a destination that blends stunning nature, rich history, and a lively culture. Whether you love outdoor adventures, history, great food, or just a peaceful getaway, Annecy has something for you. Here are some reasons to include it on your list of places to visit.

**1. A Stunning Alpine Lake**

Lake Annecy is one of the cleanest in Europe, with crystal-clear waters surrounded by mountains. It's perfect for swimming, paddleboarding, kayaking, or even paragliding over its sparkling surface. Whether you prefer a relaxing day by the shore or an adrenaline-filled adventure, this lake is unforgettable.

**2. A Charming Old Town**

Annecy's Old Town (Vieille Ville) feels like a fairytale setting, with cobblestone streets, pastel-colored buildings, and canals often compared to Venice. Walk through its narrow alleys to discover local markets, cafés, and landmarks like the Palais de l'Île, a medieval castle sitting in the middle of a canal.

### 3. Outdoor Fun in Every Season

No matter the time of year, Annecy offers plenty of activities:

- Spring & Summer: Enjoy boating, hiking, cycling, and lakeside picnics.

- Autumn: Take in the breathtaking fall colors on scenic walks.

- Winter: Skiing and snowboarding are just a short drive away at La Clusaz and Le Grand-Bornand.

### 4. A Food Lover's Dream

Located in the Savoy (Savoie) region, Annecy is known for its hearty alpine cuisine. Must-try dishes include:

- Tartiflette – A rich dish of potatoes, Reblochon cheese, bacon, and onions.

- Fondue Savoyarde – Melted cheese served with bread, perfect for cold weather.

- Fresh Lake Fish – Served with butter and herbs, straight from Lake Annecy.

## 5. A Town Full of Festivals and Culture

Annecy hosts exciting events all year:

- Annecy International Animation Film Festival (June) – A world-famous celebration of animation.

- Fête du Lac (August) – One of Europe's biggest fireworks shows over the lake.

- Christmas Markets (December) – The town turns into a festive wonderland with lights, crafts, and seasonal treats.

## 6. Easy to Reach, Relaxing to Visit

Annecy is just 40 minutes from Geneva International Airport, making it an easy getaway. Despite its popularity, the town keeps a laid-back and welcoming atmosphere, perfect for both quick trips and extended stays.

# CHAPTER 1:

# PLANNING YOUR TRIP

A well-planned trip ensures you make the most of your time in Annecy. This chapter covers the best times to visit, transportation options, packing essentials, budget tips, and other key details to help you prepare.

## Best Time to Visit

Annecy is a year-round destination, but the best time to go depends on what you want to do.

- **Spring (March-May):** Mild weather, fewer crowds, and blooming flowers make it perfect for exploring the Old Town and enjoying outdoor activities.

- **Summer (June – August):** Peak tourist season with warm temperatures, ideal for swimming, boating, and major festivals like the Annecy International Animation Film Festival (June) and the Fête du Lac (August).

- **Autumn (September – November):** Fewer tourists, cool weather, and stunning fall colors make it great for hiking and sightseeing.

- Winter (December – February): A festive atmosphere with Christmas markets, holiday lights, and easy access to ski resorts like La Clusaz and Le Grand-Bornand.

# Getting to Annecy

Annecy is well-connected by air, train, and road.

- **By Air:** The nearest major airport is Geneva International Airport (GVA) in Switzerland, about 40 km (25 miles) away. From Geneva, you can reach Annecy by:

  - Bus: Direct routes take about 1 hour.

  - Train: The journey takes around 1.5 hours.

  - Car: Renting a car gives you flexibility and takes about 40 minutes via the A41 highway.

- **By Train:** Annecy has a TGV (high-speed train) station with connections from:

  - Paris: Around 3 hours 40 minutes.

  - Lyon: roughly two hours

  - Chambéry: Around 45 minutes.

- **By Car:** The A41 highway connects Annecy to cities like Lyon and Geneva. Parking in the Old Town is limited, but public garages are available.

# Getting Around Annecy

Navigating Annecy is easy, with several transport options:

- **Walking:** The best way to explore the Old Town, as most attractions are close together.

- **Biking:** Annecy has dedicated cycling paths, especially around the lake. Rentals are available through Vélonecy.

- **Buses:** Operated by SIBRA, buses offer an affordable way to reach nearby areas.

- **Boat Tours:** A scenic way to enjoy Lake Annecy and visit lakeside villages.

- **Car Rental:** Useful for trips to the Alps or nearby ski resorts.

## What to Pack

Your packing list depends on the season, but here are some must-haves:

- Comfortable walking shoes.

- A light rain jacket (weather can be unpredictable).

- A reusable water bottle (tap water is clean and free).

- Travel adapter (if coming from outside Europe).

**- Summer (June – August):**

- Sunscreen, sunglasses, and light clothing.

- A lakeside swimsuit.

- Hiking shoes for mountain trails.

**- Winter (December – February):**

- Warm clothing, including a coat, gloves, and boots.   - Ski gear if heading to the slopes.

# Entry and Visa Information

- **EU Citizens:** No visa required.

- **US, UK, Canada, Australia:** Visa-free for stays up to 90 days in the Schengen Zone.

- **Other Nationalities:** Check the French consulate website for visa requirements.

- **Travel Insurance:** Recommended, especially for outdoor activities.

# Currency and Language

- **Currency:** Euro (€). Credit cards are widely accepted, but having some cash is useful for small purchases.

- **Language:** Although English is widely spoken in tourist areas, French is the official language.

## Budget Travel Tips

Annecy can be pricey, but you can save money with these tips:

- Visit in the shoulder seasons (spring or fall) for lower accommodation rates.

- Stay in budget-friendly hotels, hostels, or Airbnb.

- Enjoy free activities like walking tours, lake swims, and hiking trails.

- Buy food from local markets and bakeries instead of dining out for every meal.

## Money-Saving Hacks

- Book train tickets early for the best prices.

- Use public transport or rent a bike instead of taking taxis.

- Take advantage of free attractions like the Old Town and lakefront.

- Have a picnic by the lake instead of dining at expensive restaurants.

# Where to Book Your Trip

For the best deals on flights, hotels, and activities, check out:

- **Flights:** Skyscanner, Google Flights, Kayak

- **Hotels:** Booking.com, Expedia, Airbnb

- **Train Tickets:** SNCF (French National Rail)

- **Car Rentals:** Rentalcars.com, Europcar

- **Activities & Tours:** GetYourGuide, Viator

With the right planning, Annecy can be both an affordable and unforgettable trip. The next chapter will help you dive deeper into everything this charming town has to offer.

# CHAPTER 2:

# TOP ATTRACTIONS AND LANDMARKS

Annecy combines rich history with natural beauty. Here's a guide to the essential sites that make this town a favorite destination.

# 1. Old Town (Vieille Ville) – The City Center

The historic Old Town charms visitors with its stone streets, vibrant facades, and winding waterways.

- Wander narrow lanes lined with cafés, boutique shops, and local markets.

- Discover Rue Sainte-Claire, known for its arched walkways and historic buildings.

- Check out the Sunday Market for local cheeses, fresh produce, and pastries.

Highlights: A compact area that blends history, shopping, and local culture.

## 2. Palais de l'Île – An Iconic Landmark

This 12th-century building, set in the middle of the Thiou Canal, has served as a prison, courthouse, and administrative center. Today, it houses a museum that tells the town's medieval story.

Highlights: One of Annecy's most photographed and historically significant sites.

## 3. Château d'Annecy – A Castle with a View

Once the residence of the Counts of Geneva, this castle features medieval towers, Renaissance rooms, and an art museum. Its location offers clear views of the town and lake.

Highlights: A striking mix of history, architecture, and scenic vistas.

# 4. Lake Annecy – A Pristine Water Gem

Renowned for its clear waters, the lake offers a variety of activities:

- Relax at Plage de l'Impérial or Plage d'Albigny.

- Choose from boat rides, kayaking, paddleboarding, or pedaling along the shore.

- Ride a bike on the 42-km path that circles the lake.

- For the adventurous, paragliding provides a unique view from above.

Highlights: A versatile destination for both relaxation and outdoor fun.

## 5. Pont des Amours (Lovers' Bridge) – A Romantic Spot

Connecting Jardins de l'Europe with Pâquier Park, this charming footbridge provides lovely views of the lake and mountains.

- Local lore claims that a kiss here secures lasting love.

Highlights: A picturesque location perfect for couples and photography enthusiasts.

## 6. Jardins de l'Europe – A Relaxing Green Space

This park, located by the lake, features open lawns, tree-lined paths, and benches that overlook the water—ideal for a quiet break.

Highlights: A peaceful retreat for a picnic or a relaxing read.

## 7. The Thiou Canal – A Waterway with Character

Flowing through the Old Town, the Thiou Canal adds charm to the area.

- Walk along its flower-framed bridges and enjoy the reflections of the colorful buildings in the water.

Highlights: A calm spot for strolls and photography.

# 8. Basilica of the Visitation – A Spiritual and Architectural Gem

Perched on a hill, this 19th-century church features a neo-Gothic design and stunning stained-glass windows.

- Its elevated position offers clear views of the town and lake.

Highlights: A blend of art, history, and impressive vistas.

## 9. Mont Veyrier – A Hiker's Viewpoint

A hike of about 2–3 hours round trip brings you to one of the best viewpoints around Annecy.

- Enjoy sweeping scenes of the lake, town, and surrounding Alps.

Highlights: A rewarding trail for those who appreciate nature and panoramic views.

# 10. Day Trips from Annecy

If you have extra time, consider exploring these nearby spots:

- Talloires: A quiet lakeside village with notable dining options.

- Gorges du Fier: A canyon with wooden walkways set above a rushing river.

- La Clusaz & Le Grand-Bornand: Areas known for winter sports and summer hikes.

Highlights: Nearby destinations that add variety to your visit.

This guide covers the top attractions that showcase Annecy's rich history and scenic charm. Whether you're exploring ancient streets or enjoying outdoor activities, each site offers its unique appeal.

# CHAPTER 3: ACCOMMODATION OPTIONS

Finding a place to stay in Annecy is key to a smooth trip. The town offers a range of lodging choices—from luxury hotels to budget hostels—that suit various tastes and budgets. This guide breaks down the different options, highlights top hotels and affordable choices, and shares useful booking tips.

# Types of Accommodations Available

Annecy offers several lodging styles, including:

**1. Luxury Hotels & Resorts** – Upscale properties with refined service, lake views, and spa facilities.

**2. Boutique Hotels** – Small properties with a distinctive atmosphere and personalized care.

**3. Mid-Range Hotels** – Comfortable stays that balance quality amenities and cost.

**4. Budget Hotels & Hostels** – Ideal for travelers keeping an eye on expenses.

**5. Vacation Rentals & Airbnbs** – Suitable for families or groups needing extra space.

**6. Bed & Breakfasts (Chambres d'Hôtes)** – Homely stays with a local flavor.

**7. Camping & Lodges** – A choice for outdoor lovers looking to be close to nature.

# Top Hotels and Resorts (Luxury & Mid-Range Options)

### 1. Impérial Palace (★★★★★)

- Why Stay Here? Known for its striking lake views, spa services, and fine dining.

- Best For: Luxury travelers, couples, and special celebrations.

- Location: Directly on the shores of Lake Annecy.

### 2. Lake & Spa Resort Les Trésoms (★★★★)

- Why Stay Here? Offers a refined setting with spa treatments, gourmet meals, and scenic lake vistas.

- Best For: Couples and wellness seekers.

- Location: A short walk from the historic center, situated on a quiet hill.

### 3. Hôtel Le Pélican (★★★★)

- Why Stay Here? A modern property with spacious rooms and top-notch amenities.

- Best For: Families and business travelers.

- Location: Close to both the lake and the city center.

## 4. Hôtel du Palais de l'Isle (★★★)

- Why Stay Here? A cozy hotel in the heart of the Old Town, offering views of the Thiou Canal.

- Best For: History enthusiasts and those looking for authentic local charm.

- Location: Next to the well-known Palais de l'Île.

# Budget-Friendly Options (Affordable Stays)

### 1. Ibis Annecy Centre Vieille Ville (★★★)

- Why Stay Here? A budget-friendly hotel praised for its clean and comfortable rooms.

- Best For: Cost-conscious travelers wanting to be near the Old Town.

- Location: A brief walk from the main attractions.

### 2. Hôtel des Alpes (★★)

- Why Stay Here? Provides simple yet cozy accommodations without breaking the bank.

- Best For: Solo travelers and couples seeking a central stay.

- Location: Near the train station and within walking distance of Lake Annecy.

### 3. Auberge de Jeunesse Annecy (Hostel)

- Why Stay Here? The city's only youth hostel, ideal for social backpackers.

- Best For: Solo adventurers, backpackers, and small groups.

- Location: Roughly 20 minutes by foot or bus from the Old Town.

## 4. Camping International du Lac Bleu (Camping & Budget Lodges)

- Why Stay Here? Perfect for nature fans, with options to rent cabins or camp by the water.

- Best For: Outdoor enthusiasts and those on a budget.

- Location: About a 15-minute drive from Annecy, near the lake.

# Tips for Booking and Choosing Accommodation

### 1. Book Early in Peak Seasons

Annecy is busy in summer (June–August) and winter (December–February). Reserving your stay 2–3 months in advance can secure better rates.

### 2. Consider Location

- For exploring the Old Town, choose lodging near Vieille Ville or the city center.

- If you prefer a quieter setting, opt for properties by the lake or in areas like Talloires.

- For ski trips, select accommodations near transit options for easy access to resorts.

### 3. Compare Prices on Booking Sites

Use platforms like Booking.com, Expedia, Hotels.com, or Airbnb to find competitive rates and special offers.

### 4. Check Reviews Before Booking

Read guest feedback on sites such as TripAdvisor, Google Reviews, or Booking.com to ensure the property meets your standards.

## 5. Look for Complimentary Perks

Some properties offer extras like free breakfast, Wi-Fi, or bike rentals, which can help reduce your overall costs.

## 6. Consider Nearby Towns for Better Rates

If you're working with a tight budget, explore nearby locations like Seynod, Menthon-Saint-Bernard, or Talloires, which may offer lower prices without sacrificing convenience.

This guide helps you navigate the lodging options in Annecy, ensuring that you find a stay that matches your travel style and budget. Happy planning!

# CHAPTER 4:

# DINING AND CUISINE

Annecy blends hearty mountain ingredients with French culinary finesse. The town's menus showcase robust flavors from local farms and the lake. This guide outlines signature dishes, standout restaurants, affordable eats, lakeside dining spots, and local wine options.

# Local Cuisine and Popular Dishes

Situated in the Haute-Savoie region, Annecy is known for filling, rustic fare. Be sure to try:

**1. Tartiflette**

A warming dish of potatoes, melted Reblochon cheese, onions, and bacon.

**2. Raclette**

Melted semi-hard cheese poured over boiled potatoes, cured meats, and pickles—often prepared at the table.

**3. Fondue Savoyarde**

A blend of Comté, Beaufort, and Tomme de Savoie cheeses served with bread cubes for dipping.

**4. Diots and Polenta**

Savoyard sausages simmered in white wine or onions, paired with polenta or potatoes.

**5. Féra and Omble Chevalier**

Fresh lake fish that is typically grilled or lightly cooked in butter.

## 6. Gâteau de Savoie

A light, airy sponge cake frequently served with fruit or jam.

## 7. Crozets de Savoie

Small, square-shaped pasta made from buckwheat or wheat flour, often baked with cheese.

# Best Restaurants in Annecy (For All Budgets)

**1. Le Clos des Sens (Three Michelin Stars)**

Offers innovative dishes inspired by local ingredients along with views of the lake.

**2. L'Etage**

A cozy spot with wooden interiors serving traditional Alpine dishes like Tartiflette, Fondue, and Raclette.

**3. La Ciboulette (Michelin Star)**

Presents modern French cuisine with seasonal menus that highlight local produce.

**4. Chez Mamie Lise**

Feels like dining in a traditional Savoyard home with offerings such as Diots with polenta and hearty potato dishes.

**5. Le Freti**

A favorite for cheese lovers, specializing in Raclette and Fondue.

# Street Food and Local Eateries (Budget-Friendly Options)

## 1. Crêperie Ti Mad

Serves authentic Breton-style crêpes and galettes. Try the ham and cheese galette or a sweet Nutella crêpe.

## 2. La Buvette du Marché

Located in the Old Town Market, this eatery offers fresh sandwiches, cheese plates, and charcuterie.

## 3. Pâtisserie Philippe Rigollot

Run by a renowned pastry chef, this bakery features macarons, fruit tarts, and Gâteau de Savoie.

## 4. Les Burgers de Papa

Crafts gourmet French-style burgers using local ingredients.

# Dining by the Lake (Scenic Outdoor Options)

**1. Auberge du Père Bise (Michelin Star, Talloires)**

Enjoy a meal on the lakeside terrace while sampling specialties focused on fresh lake fish.

**2. La Brasserie des Européens**

A casual spot on the waterfront known for its fresh fish and seafood platters.

**3. Restaurant Le Belvédère**

Offers relaxed dining on a hill with clear, panoramic views of the lake.

**4. Le Café de l'Abbaye (Talloires)**

A quiet venue near the Abbey of Talloires serves straightforward, fresh dishes.

Annecy's dining scene caters to every palate and budget, showcasing a rich mix of traditional Alpine recipes and refined French cooking. Enjoy exploring the flavors that make this town a culinary highlight.

# CHAPTER 5:

# OUTDOOR ACTIVITIES AND ADVENTURE

Annecy is a hub for outdoor pursuits, with activities ranging from peaceful hikes and scenic bike rides to water sports and daring challenges. The striking Alpine backdrop and crystal-clear lake set the stage for both relaxed days and high-energy outings. Here's a guide to the top outdoor adventures in Annecy.

# Hiking Trails Galore

Surrounded by impressive Alpine scenery, Annecy offers trails that suit every level:

**1. Mont Veyrier et Mont Baron**

- Overview: A popular route with sweeping views of Lake Annecy and the surrounding peaks.

- Level: Moderate (approximately 3–4 hours round trip).

- Starting Point: Parking du Col des Contrebandiers, about a 10-minute drive from town.

**2. La Tournette**

- Overview: Climb to the highest peak above Annecy (2,351 m) for a full-circle view of the town, Mont Blanc, and the Alps.

- Level: Challenging (6–8 hours round trip with steep sections).

- Starting Point: Chalet de l'Aulp near Montmin.

### 3. Roc de Chère Nature Reserve

- Overview: A gentle, family-friendly walk with pleasant views of Lake Annecy.

- Level: Easy (1–2 hours round trip).

- Starting Point: Close to Talloires, about 20 minutes from Annecy.

### 4. Cascade dragon

- Overview: A short trail that leads to a lovely waterfall.

- Level: Easy to moderate (roughly 1.5 hours round trip).

- Starting Point: In the area near Talloires.

# Boat Tours and Water Adventures

Lake Annecy ranks among Europe's cleanest, inviting you to explore its waters by various means:

**1. Lake Annecy Boat Tours**

- Overview: Cruise along the lake to view its charm and nearby villages.

- Options:

  - Large boat cruises with regional commentary

  - Private rentals (self-drive or with a captain)

  - Taxi boats for a quick, scenic ride

- Recommended Provider: Compagnie des Bateaux du Lac d'Annecy.

**2. Kayaking & Paddleboarding**

- Overview: Navigate the lake at your own pace to uncover hidden coves and quiet spots.

- Rental Options: Annecy Lake Kayak and Roul'Ma Poule (which also offers bike rentals).

## 3. Paragliding Over the Lake

- Overview: Glide above the lake and mountains for striking aerial views.

- Providers: Takamaka and K2 Parapente.

# Cycling Through the Countryside

Annecy's well-maintained bike paths and mountain trails make it a delight for cyclists:

**1. Annecy Lake Bike Path (Voie Verte)**

- Overview: A 42-km loop along the lake that showcases scenic views.

- Level: Easy, flat, and suited for all riders.

- Rentals: Vélonecy and Roul'Ma Poule.

**2. Col de la Forclaz**

- Overview: A steep mountain climb that rewards riders with a stunning view of the lake below.

- Level: Difficult; a challenge for road cyclists.

**3. Mountain Biking in Semnoz**

- Overview: Tackle downhill trails that wind through forests with glimpses of the lake.

- Best Season: Summer, when ski lifts help transport bikes to the slopes.

# Beach Bliss

Several beaches in and around Annecy offer spots to swim, sunbathe, or picnic:

### 1. Plage dealign

   - Overview: A spacious, grassy beach with easy access to the lake and nearby eateries.

   - Location: About a 15-minute walk from the Old Town.

### 2. Plage de l'Impérial

   - Overview: A lively beach complete with a floating water park, volleyball courts, and snack bars.

   - Note: There is a small entry fee during the summer months.

### 3. Angon Beach

   - Overview: A quieter option featuring sandy shores and shallow waters, ideal for families.

- Location: Near Talloires, roughly a 25-minute drive from Annecy.

# Rock Climbing and Adventure Sports

For those seeking a rush, Annecy provides options for climbing and other adventure sports:

**1. Via Ferrata du Roc de Cornillon**

- Overview: A guided climbing route equipped with ladders and cables, suited to beginners.

- Level: Easy to moderate (harness required).

- Location: Near Aix-les-Bains, about 45 minutes from Annecy.

**2. Canyoning in Angon or Montmin**

- Overview: Tackle gorges with jumps, slides, and waterfall descents for a refreshing thrill.

- Providers: Takamaka Annecy and Annecy Canyoning.

**3. Rock Climbing in Grand Bornand**

- Overview: Challenge yourself on quality limestone routes that provide dramatic Alpine backdrops.

- Level: Designed for seasoned climbers.

Whether you prefer a gentle stroll, a vigorous bike ride, or an adrenaline-fueled climb, Annecy's outdoor offerings cater to every taste and skill level. Enjoy the natural beauty and active lifestyle that make this region a favorite among adventurers.

# CHAPTER 6:
# ART, CULTURE, AND ENTERTAINMENT

Annecy goes beyond its scenic views and outdoor thrills by offering a lively cultural scene. The town boasts a calendar full of festivals, art galleries, museums, and diverse nightlife options. This guide highlights the events, cultural spots, shopping areas, and places to unwind after dark.

# Local Festivals and Events

Annecy hosts some of France's most notable festivals. Mark your calendar for these key events:

## 1. Annecy International Animation Film Festival (June)

- Highlights: The world's largest animation festival, featuring film premieres, workshops, and open-air screenings.

- Venues: Multiple sites including Bonlieu Scène Nationale and outdoor spots by the lake.

- Tip: Reserve tickets early as this event attracts visitors from all over.

## 2. Fête du Lac (First Saturday of August)

- Highlights: One of Europe's grandest fireworks displays set over the lake, accompanied by music and light shows.

- Best Viewing: Pâquier Park or a boat on Lake Annecy.

- Advice: To guarantee a decent place, arrive early.

### 3. Descente des Alpages (October)

- Highlights: A celebration of mountain traditions with a parade of cows, local music, and food stalls offering regional specialties.

- Annecy Old Town is the location.

- Tip: Sample the local cheese and sausage treats available at the stalls.

### 4. Christmas Markets (December)

- Highlights: A festive winter setting complete with twinkling lights, mulled wine, and handcrafted gifts.

- Locations: Place François de Menthon and throughout the Old Town.

- Tip: Visit after dark for a magical atmosphere and a warm hot tartiflette.

# Art Galleries and Museums

Discover Annecy's creative side with a mix of historic sites and contemporary art spaces:

**1. Château d'Annecy – Museum of Annecy**

   - Highlights: A medieval castle that houses exhibits on local history, fine art, and modern pieces.

   - Location: Perched on a hill overlooking the Old Town.

   - Tip: Visit the terrace for panoramic views of the city.

**2. Palais de l'Île – Annecy's Landmark**

   - Highlights: A 12th-century building in the middle of a canal, now serving as a museum focused on the town's past.

   - Tip: Perfect for photography enthusiasts due to its striking architecture.

**3. Musée du Film d'Animation**

- Highlights: A compact museum dedicated to the history of animated films, situated within the Château d'Annecy.

- Tip: An ideal stop during the International Animation Festival.

**4. Galerie Art By Friends**

- Highlights: A modern gallery showcasing street art, photography, and pop culture exhibits.

- Near the train station is the location.

# Shopping and Markets

Annecy offers a range of shopping opportunities, from bustling markets to chic boutiques:

## 1. Old Town Market (Tuesdays, Fridays & Sundays)

- Highlights: A lively market selling fresh cheese, sausages, pastries, and handmade crafts.

- Location: Spread through the winding streets of the Old Town.

- Tip: Don't leave without picking up some Reblochon cheese.

## 2. Rue Royale & Courier Shopping Center

- Highlights: The main shopping corridor features French fashion, cafés, and popular high-street stores like Sephora, Zara, and FNAC.

## 3. La Vieille Usine (Concept Store)

- Highlights: A boutique offering handmade furniture, vintage décor, and locally produced crafts.

## 4. Chocolaterie Meyer

- Highlights: An artisan chocolate shop known for its handmade truffles and pralines—perfect for gifts or a sweet treat.

# Nightlife and Entertainment Options

While Annecy isn't known for a wild party scene, it has plenty of spots for a pleasant evening out:

**1. Le Munich**

   - Highlights: A popular beer bar offering a wide selection of local and international brews, with views over Pâquier Park and the lake.

**2. Captain Pub**

   - Highlights: A British-style pub known for its cozy ambiance, good beer, and live sports broadcasts.

   - The Old Town is the location.

**3. Pop Plage**

   - Highlights: A stylish nightclub by the lake featuring DJs, creative cocktails, and a lively dance floor with scenic views.

**4. Le 27 Bar**

- Highlights: A chic cocktail bar offering inventive drinks in an intimate setting.

**5. Casino Impérial**

- Highlights: Located inside the Impérial Palace Hotel, this venue combines gaming with an elegant dining setting.

Annecy's cultural and entertainment scene offers a rich variety of events and venues that cater to every interest. Whether you're drawn to festivals, museums, boutique shopping, or a relaxed evening at a local bar, the town provides plenty of options to enjoy your downtime.

# CHAPTER 7:

# A 7-DAY ITINERARY IN ANNECY

Plan your week-long visit to Annecy with this organized itinerary that covers everything from scenic hikes and boat trips to cultural visits and local dining. The schedule is broken into morning, afternoon, and evening plans to help you see the town's top sights while leaving time to relax in this charming Alpine setting.

# Day 1:

# Getting There and Seeing the Old Town

**Morning: Arrival**

- Arrive via Geneva International Airport (a 40-minute transfer by shuttle, train, or car) or take a direct train from cities such as Paris or Lyon.

- Check into your hotel—staying in or near the Old Town makes most attractions easily accessible on foot.

**Afternoon: Old Town Walk**

- Begin on Rue Sainte-Claire, where you'll find quaint boutiques, archways, and cafés.

- Stop by the iconic Palais de l'Île, a 12th-century structure set in a canal.

- Wander along the Thiou Canal, taking in the picturesque bridges and waterways.

- Enjoy lunch at a local spot like Chez Mamie Lise, known for its traditional tartiflette.

**Evening: Lakeside Stroll & Dinner**

- Walk through Jardins de l'Europe along the lakefront.

- Cross the Pont des Amours to catch a beautiful sunset.

- Dine at Le Belvédère, which offers sweeping views of the lake.

# Day 2:

# Outdoor Adventures & Boat Cruise

**Morning: Hike or Bike**

- Tackle a moderate 3-hour hike up Mont Veyrier to see expansive views of Lake Annecy.

- Alternatively, rent a bicycle and ride along the lake's edge.

**Afternoon: On the Water**

- Set off on a one-hour boat tour with Compagnie des Bateaux to get a different view of the lake and nearby villages.

- Rent a kayak or paddleboard from Roul'Ma Poule to explore at your own pace.

- Pause for a picnic at Plage d'Albigny.

**Evening: Local Fare & Wine**

- Head to Le Freti for a hearty meal featuring raclette or fondue.

- Follow up with a wine-tasting session at Le Vin Chez Moi to sample regional Savoie wines.

# Day 3:

# Château Visits & Cycling the Countryside

### Morning: History & Markets

- Visit Château d'Annecy, a medieval castle now serving as a museum that details the town's history.

- Browse the Old Town Market (open Tuesday, Friday, and Sunday) for local cheeses, pastries, and charcuterie.

### Afternoon: Bike Ride to Talloires

- Rent a bike and follow the Voie Verte cycle path to Talloires.

- Tour the charming Château de Menthon-Saint-Bernard, a storybook castle set against the countryside.

## Evening: Dinner with a View

- Enjoy dinner in Talloires at Auberge du Père Bise, a Michelin-rated restaurant with lakeside seating.

- Return to Annecy by boat taxi for a relaxing end to the day.

# Day 4:

# Day Trip to La Clusaz & Alpine Activities

### Morning: Short Drive & Gondola Ride

- Drive about 30 minutes to La Clusaz, a picturesque Alpine village.

- Take the gondola up to the Beauregard Plateau for impressive mountain vistas.

### Afternoon: Mountain Fun

- Try your hand at paragliding or summer tobogganing.

- Enjoy a filling Savoyard lunch at a mountain chalet such as La Ferme.

### Evening: Casual Return

- Head back to Annecy and take a leisurely walk along the lake promenade.

- Choose a relaxed dinner at Brasserie des Européens, known for its fresh seafood.

# Day 5:

# Art, Culture & Shopping

### Morning: Museums & Landmarks

- Visit the Musée-Château d'Annecy to view historical and art exhibits.

- Stop by Palais de l'Île to appreciate its architectural charm and local history.

### Afternoon: Retail Therapy

- Shop along Rue Royale and at local markets for French fashion, souvenirs, and gourmet treats.

- Pick up artisan chocolates at Chocolaterie Meyer and sample local cheese from La Fromagerie.

### Evening: Night Out

- Start the evening with a cocktail at Le 27 Bar.

- Later, head to Pop Plage, a stylish lakeside club that plays music and offers a lively atmosphere.

# Day 6:

# Lakeside Relaxation & Hidden Spots

**Morning: Nature Walk**

- Visit the Roc de Chère Nature Reserve for an easy walk that offers lovely views of the lake and surrounding scenery.

**Afternoon: Beach Time & Water Sports**

- Swim at Angon Beach, a quieter spot away from the crowds.

- For more excitement, try wakeboarding or waterskiing at Gliss'Cool.

**Evening: Dinner & Games**

- Dine at L'Atelier Gourmand, a favorite among locals for its warm, home-style cooking.

- Cap off the night with a visit to Casino Impérial.

# Day 7:

# Farewell to Annecy

**Morning: Brunch & Final Stroll**

- Enjoy a relaxed brunch at Café Bunna.

- Take one last walk along the Thiou Canal, soaking in the town's charm.

**Afternoon: Departure**

- If you're flying from Geneva, leave with ample time for your transfer.

- For train travelers, grab a final pastry from Philippe Rigollot as a sweet send-off before departing.

This seven-day itinerary covers Annecy's highlights and offers a balanced mix of history, natural beauty, local cuisine, and leisure activities. Use it to guide your journey through one of the Alps' most picturesque towns.

# CHAPTER 8:

# PRACTICAL INFORMATION AND TIPS

Before you set out for Annecy, it's helpful to review local customs, language basics, safety guidelines, and handy travel tools. This chapter offers clear advice on manners, communication, health, and useful resources to make your visit smooth.

# Etiquette and Customs

In Annecy, courteous behavior is important. Keep these pointers in mind:

### Greetings & Social Behavior

- When entering a shop, restaurant, or hotel, greet with a friendly "Bonjour" or "Bonsoir."

- A simple "Merci" and "Au revoir" when leaving is appreciated.

- Among friends, a light kiss on each cheek is common; for new acquaintances, a handshake works best.

### Dining Rules

- Wait for the host's "Bon appétit" before beginning your meal.

- A tip isn't required as service charges are included, though leaving a small gratuity (around 5–10%) is welcomed.

- Keep voices low while dining to maintain a relaxed atmosphere.

**Public Behavior**

- Speak softly on public transport, in museums, and eateries.

- Avoid eating while walking; meals are meant to be enjoyed while seated.

- Greet shopkeepers when you enter small stores.

**Dress Code**

- Choose smart casual attire. Although Annecy is relaxed, avoid sportswear in restaurants unless you're at a ski resort.

# Language and Communication

French is the official language in Annecy. While many locals in tourist areas speak some English, knowing a few basic phrases will help you get around and show respect.

**Useful French Phrases**

Greetings & Basic Conversation

- Bonjour – Hello

- Bonsoir – Good evening

- Merci – Thank you

- S'il vous plaît – Please

- Excusez-moi – Excuse me

- Sure/No - Oui/Non

Ordering Food & Drinks

- Je voudrais, or "I'd like," Additionally, if it's okay with you, the bill - "A café, s'il vous plaît" means

"Please, a coffee." If it's okay with you, might we have a table for two?

Asking for Directions

- Où est…? – Where is…?

- À gauche / À droite – Left / Right

- Tout droit – Straight ahead

- Parlez-vous anglais? – Do you speak English?

Transportation

- Où est la gare? – Where is the train station?

- Combien coûte un billet pour…? – How much is a ticket to…?

- À quelle heure part le train? – What time does the train leave?

Emergency Phrases

- Appelez une ambulance! – Call an ambulance!

- J'ai besoin d'aide: I require assistance.

- Où est la pharmacie la plus proche? – Where is the nearest pharmacy?

Tip: If you're unsure about pronunciation, apps like Google Translate or Duolingo can be very useful.

# Health and Safety Tips

Annecy is a safe destination, but a few precautions can help:

**Health & Medical Care**

- Pharmacies are well-stocked, and pharmacists can provide basic advice.

- For medical needs, ask your hotel for a "Médecin Généraliste."

- Travelers from the EU can use their European Health Insurance Card (EHIC); non-EU visitors should carry travel insurance.

Personal Safety

- While pickpocketing is uncommon, keep your belongings secure in busy areas.

- Be cautious in isolated areas near the lake after dark.

- When hiking, check the weather, and bring a map, water, and a fully charged phone.

# Emergency Contacts

Save these numbers on your phone for quick reference:

- Emergency Services (Police, Fire, Ambulance): 112 (EU-wide)

- Local Police (Gendarmerie): +33 4 50 33 78 00

- Annecy Hospital (Hôpital d'Annecy-Genevois): +33 4 50 63 63 63

- Pharmacy Emergency: Dial 3237 to locate the nearest open pharmacy

- Lost or Stolen Credit Cards: Contact your bank's international helpline immediately

# Communication and Internet Access

## SIM Cards & Mobile Data

- Consider purchasing a local SIM card from providers like Orange, SFR, or Bouygues Telecom, available at kiosks or supermarkets.

- Alternatively, an eSIM service (such as Airalo) allows you to avoid swapping cards.

- Many hotels, cafés, and restaurants offer free Wi-Fi, though quality may vary.

Wi-Fi Availability

- Public spaces, such as train stations and tourist offices, usually have free Wi-Fi.

- When dining, ask if the café or restaurant provides Wi-Fi access.

## Useful Apps, Websites, and Maps

Equip yourself with these tools for a hassle-free visit:

- Navigation: Use Google Maps for real-time directions or Maps.me for offline routes.

- Public Transport: The SIBRA App helps with bus schedules in Annecy.

- Bike Rentals: Vélonecy is a convenient option for renting bikes.

- Translation: Google Translate offers text and voice translation; Duolingo can help you learn basic French.

- Dining Reservations: The Fork (La Fourchette) is great for booking tables.

- Activity Booking: Platforms like GetYourGuide and Viator list tours and boat cruises.

- Medical Services: Doctolib helps you find and book a doctor if necessary.

- Pharmacy Finder: Use 3237.fr to locate nearby open pharmacies.

With these practical tips and resources, you're well-prepared to navigate Annecy smoothly. This guide aims to simplify your planning, help you interact respectfully, and keep you safe during your visit. Enjoy your journey!

# CONCLUSION:

# YOUR ANNECY ADVENTURES AWAITS

We've reached the end of this guide, and I hope you feel ready to explore Annecy—a destination where history, nature, adventure, and culture blend in perfect harmony. Whether you plan to stroll through the charming Old Town, sail on a clear lake, hike scenic mountain trails, or sample hearty Alpine dishes, Annecy offers moments and memories that last well beyond your visit.

This guide has introduced you to top attractions, practical travel tips, local customs, and secret spots that make Annecy truly special. You now know the best times to visit, how to get around, where to stay, and what to eat. All that remains is to put your plans into action.

Remember, travel isn't just about checking off sights—it's about the people you meet and the memories you build. Whether you're planning a solo trip, a romantic retreat, or a family vacation, let this guide serve as your starting point. Don't hesitate to stray from the usual routes, try new ideas, and welcome surprises along the way.

Annecy has a way of winning hearts with its timeless beauty and friendly spirit. Once you visit, you might find yourself longing to return. So book that ticket, pack your bags, and begin your journey—Annecy is waiting for you.

Bon voyage et à bientôt! (Safe travels and see you soon!)

Made in United States
Cleveland, OH
18 March 2025